THE SCIENCE BEHIND WISDOM

K.D.Amerson

Copyright © 2021 K.D.Amerson

To Byb, the other member of our little sangha...

CONTENTS

THE POWER OF THE PRESENT MOMENT

Finding Inner Peace and Optimizing Potential

'Look past your thoughts, so you may drink the pure nectar of This Moment." - Rumi

This book examines the science behind ancient meditative techniques and shows why these philosophies and practices are so effective in improving our mental health, well-being, and even cognitive performance.
The ancient masters had an incredible understanding of human psychology, learned through observation and analysis. Many of their observations and conclusions were obviously sound because modern psychotherapy regularly uses these concepts in the therapeutic process.

One of the most well-known concepts currently is 'mindfulness' or keeping your attention in the present moment, which has been advocated by teachers of many different ancient spiritual paths including Taoism, Hinduism, and Buddhism.

It has been discovered that following mindfulness techniques have not only had an extremely positive impact on people's mental health and well being but also on their ability to problem solve and complete tasks successfully.

For example, monks who regularly practiced mindfulness underwent laboratory tests that indicated their brains showed higher levels of Gamma oscillations.

Gamma is the fastest brainwave frequency and is an indication that *all parts of the brain are working in harmony* to make decisions or problem solve. Higher levels of gamma waves lead to improved sensory perception and recall, as well as increased focus, brain processing speed, and concentration, and are associated with peak levels of cognitive functioning. Individuals with higher levels of gamma are often highly intelligent, happy, and compassionate, with excellent memories.

This proves that mindfulness and living in the present can help improve our mental health while increasing our capabilities and the possibility of reaching our potential. Obviously, this is a massive win-win, but requires us to let go of negative thought processes that take us away from the present and which are often purely *imagined* concepts.

For instance, how often have we taken ourselves out of the present by becoming preoccupied with think-

ing that people would react to us in a negative way, but they didn't, or believed that something would go wrong, and it hasn't. Yet we have suffered dreadfully while imagining that awful things would occur.
When we dwell on imagined future negative situations it is as though our bodies are existing in a comfortable reality in the present, but we have projected our minds into the future to an apocalyptic world where we live an unhappy existence that has never happened, or perhaps projected our thoughts back into the past to a troubling time that happened long ago.
If we are lucky enough to have enough food and a safe warm place to stay why allow phantoms and imagined horrors to cause us mental pain and destroy our reality in the now?
As Mark Twain insightfully said – *"I am an old man and I have known many troubles, but most of them never happened."*

From a purely practical standpoint, while these thoughts occupy our mind, they often prevent us from concentrating on any other tasks or processing information and problem solving effectively, preventing us from achieving our goals. Therefore, allowing these mental constructs and phantoms of fear to control our mind causes us pain and seriously limits our potential.
By staying mentally rooted in the present, it is possible to remain focused on tasks or problem solving

for better results and helps to prevent the mind being drawn into negative thoughts and depression.
The next sections look at techniques that help achieve a mindful state in our normal daily lives and explain the neurological and psychological reasons they are so effective.

THE POWER OF RECOGNITION

Preventing Negative Thoughts from Controlling Your Mind

"Liberation occurs from recognising just that by which we are bound." - Ninth Gyalwang Karmapa

Because our own thoughts and anxiety often prevent us from living mindfully in the present, Ayurvedic and Buddhist practioners recommend the use of 'thought recognition', to release or detach clinging or repeating thoughts, i.e., recognising thoughts so that they naturally fall away and are released.

These practices conclude that the most persistent negative thoughts can lead to even more negative thoughts, until we are drawn down the rabbit hole of stress and obsession, and are caused by *aversion* (fear and anxiety, or anger) or *craving* (desire or addiction).

By staying conscious of our thoughts in this form of continuous, gentle, state of awareness we can dispel aversive or craving thoughts by calmly mentally recognising them as '*an aversion*' or '*a craving*' without feeling irritation or judgement towards ourselves.
This prevents us from being lost in negative thoughts that take us away from the present and helps to move along unwanted thoughts that have hooked into our consciousness, causing mental suffering. In this way we can stay in the present doing our jobs or pastimes, while maintaining a gentle awareness that recognises and releases the thoughts that become "hooked" or "stuck".
Often the reason negative thoughts persist is because the aversion or fear these thoughts trigger engage the Amygdala, the area of the brain associated with fight or flight.
Scientists have discovered that there is a link between the parasympathetic nervous system, the lower nodes of the lungs, and the Amygdala - so a low placed, gentle breath, will indicate to the amygdala that you are safe, and it can de-activate. Therefore, in conjunction with the thought recognition exercise described above it helps to take a low-placed, gentle, deep breath that reaches to the bottom of your lungs at the same time.

Most ancient meditation techniques, including Yoga, employ deep breathing as part of their processes, as although they might not have been aware of the

neurological reasons for the relaxing properties of a deep breath, they observed its effectiveness by experience.
Even western society understood its value in helping individuals to calm themselves and make reasoned decisions, shown by the old saying -
"Take a deep breath and count to ten."
This would be suggested to someone before they spoke or made a decision if they were angry or upset. Wise advice to help calm the person before things were said and done in an aversive state, that they might later...

To achieve a low centred breath visualise you are softly, and gently, breathing up through your feet and legs, as well as through your belly button and into your lower back. It is important to have the mouth slightly open and your jaw relaxed, as you gently take in the air. A forced heavy deep breath will only feel like a panicked breath so a deep, gentle, sigh-like breath will be far more calming. It also helps to place one hand on your chest and another on the lower abdomen as you breath in. If the chest stays still, while your lower abdomen expands and moves, it will show you have taken a low breath correctly.
By recognising and releasing your clinging negative thoughts as 'aversion or craving', along with taking a low centred breath, the thoughts should immediately detach and move on. If they return, gently repeat the same process until they clear, and you can re-

turn to mindfully attending to your job, or pastime.

This is a powerful, yet subtle, form of continual awareness meditation that helps us return to a mindful state whenever our thoughts try to distract us from the present.
Considering that our brain and gamma waves function far better in this state, as well as helping us to improve our mental well-being, science certainly demonstrates these ancient techniques are worth following.

THE AMYGDALA SMOKE ALARM AND THE HIPPOCAMPUS LIBRARY

How We Pacify the Most Ancient Parts of Our Brain

"Knowing your own darkness is the best method for dealing with the darknesses of other people." Carl Gustav Jung

As mentioned in the previous section, the scientific reasons behind the effectiveness of recognition and release meditation, particularly with accompanying deep breathing, are linked to the behaviour of two of the most ancient and primitive parts of our brain – the Amygdala and Hippocampus.

It is our Amygdala and Hippocampus that initially set up a feeling of anxiety regarding our surroundings and situations, as they try to warn us of possible danger.

The Hippocampus takes mental pictures and stores memories of previously upsetting situations and places. It then initiates hormone release from a part of the brain called the hypothalamus to alert the Amygdala when it recognises a place or situation that it has recorded as a threat. Even a thought about an upsetting situation can cause it to react.

The Amygdala behaves just like a smoke alarm which sounds out whether it senses the harmless smoke from burnt toast or from a serious fire. It will set off a neurological reaction as soon as it senses the warning hormones.

Often the situations they are alerting us to are not life threatening in modern day living but will appear dangerous to these ancient and mostly instinctive parts of our brain, which developed long before we had language.

When alerted to danger our ancestors would turn and run, or fight for their lives, and this has become known as '*the fight or flight response*'. Sadly, once this response is initiated the amygdala shuts down the more complex problem-solving parts of the brain. This includes our frontal lobe which is responsible for executive functions, the highest cognitive and processing functions humans have - including the ability to plan, to organise, use expressive language, experience empathy, and flexibility of thinking.

The Amygdala shuts down more complex functions to optimise our immediate responses, like jumping out of the way of danger before we've even consciously thought about it. However, if the Amygdala mistakenly takes control during a non-life-threatening situation we struggle to give a measured or considered response to more complex situations, because we are using a limited and less advanced proportion of our brain.

When we use 'thought-recognition' to acknowledge that the situation is not an immediate threat to our lives, only an aversive thought, the Hippocampus discards the image or memory. As a result, the negative reaction to a situation or a repetitive aversive thought will often completely cease to appear in our mind from then on.
Gentle deep breathing also doubles the power of the thought-recognition, as it physically informs the non-verbal Amygdala of your safety at the same time.

As mentioned in the previous section, deep breathing is effective because a breath that reaches into the lower nodes of the lungs can activate the parasympathetic nervous system, which then releases hormones that send a signal to the brain to tell the Amygdala that you are safe and no longer need to use the '*fight or flight*' response.
This is probably because in our early stages of evolution, before we developed language, whenever our ancestors escaped from danger and felt safe their bodies would return to deep, slow, regular breath-

ing - indicating to the Amygdala that the danger had passed.

Along with the practice of recognising and releasing anxious or aversive thoughts, this will allow the accompanying dread or worry to pass immediately. It will also enable us to use the more evolved parts of our brain to problem solve more effectively. This means we can be more effective in dealing with high pressure situations like exams, interviews or negotiations and other areas requiring our best performance mentally, or physically.

At first this method of conscious recognition and deep breathing will need to be done very frequently. However, thanks to the amazing plasticity of the brain, the process soon becomes automatic. Eventually a gentle deep breath will help release the trapped or hooked thought as soon as it is noticed.

The Amygdala and Hippocampus are a valuable and important resource. They can warn you if a car is coming towards you, or if you are in any other dangerous situation. We still need them, but there are times that they over-react and take over when the circumstances are not life threatening and could be easily resolved in modern day life. Therefore, we must be able to switch them off without drama or blame, so that we can reach our full potential.

WHAT IS HIDDEN BENEATH

Acknowledging The Inner Child

"In every adult, there lurks a child – an eternal child, something that is always becoming, is never completed and calls for unceasing care, attention and education. That is the part of the human personality which wants to develop and become whole." - Carl Jung.

The process of recognition is not only helpful for repetitious individual thoughts, but also invaluable in releasing past trauma, including those experienced in childhood.
This is part of modern psychology and talking therapy, in which the subject speaks about past traumatic events to recognise them, resolve them, and finally let them go. It can also support the daily practice of thought recognition and release of more general aversive thoughts about the past, that hook into our mind and keep us from being fully present.

We can all benefit from recognising and releasing past traumatic events during our meditations rather than locking them away in corners of our minds, as they will undoubtedly manifest as unconscious behaviours and reactions to the world around us.
For those that have sadly experienced extreme trauma the support of a qualified mental health professional during this process will be necessary. However, for most people who haven't experienced extreme trauma, going to the locked corners of our mind during quiet reflection and opening the doors to release the past can be helpful.
After all, if you heard a crying child in a locked room would you shout at it to be silent, or drink until you passed out and couldn't hear it anymore? Hopefully not! You wouldn't want to be so uncaring and cruel. So why do the same to your own inner child?
In many ways the crying inner child is like the "smoke alarm" amygdala, seeking to be recognised and acknowledged. Once it is acknowledged it can often be pacified.

The inner child and your psyche can also benefit from you going a step further and befriending and caring for the echo of the child you were. Visualisations of kindly interacting with, or lovingly embracing and comforting a mental projection of the little child you were, can be very therapeutic. We can resolve and end a negative cycle by opening the locked door, leading them out into the light, and acknowledging and giving love to our own inner child that is crying out for attention.

By bringing these unconscious thought processes into our consciousness, we can lessen the aversive and reactive thoughts we experience from moment to moment and, very importantly, the way we react to others. We can cease the cycle of hidden pain causing ourselves, and others, more suffering and let go of the addictions and comforting behaviours we use to block out the cries of our inner child. Becoming free to live without suffering, in the present.

REVEALING THE UNSEEN

Bringing the Subconscious into the Light of Awareness

"Until you make the unconscious conscious it will direct your life and you will call it fate." Carl Jung

In the previous sections we explored subconscious triggers for our reactions and behaviours that can be caused by the more primitive areas of our brains, or by traumas from the past that can affect how we relate to others. Traumas which may have happened so long ago, for instance in childhood, that we are unaware they are affecting our decisions and reactions in the present.
Added to the subconscious, social, and experiential programming we operate under, there are the deeper primitive and primal instincts from our primate ancestors that also cause our reactions. It is therefore important that we recognise these to understand our primal behaviours.

For our ancient ancestors, other primates or humans

were one of the most serious dangers. Being rejected by the troop/tribe in our primate or early human past could also lead to certain death, as the collective protected us from other aggressive primates, humans, and predators. Reacting to this primitive and subconscious fear we can often engage in long internal discussions as to why another person is behaving in a negative way and think about how we can placate or defeat them.

However, the reality is that no matter how upsetting rejection by other humans is, in most modern societies rejection will not result in death, and so dwelling on the situation will only cause suffering of the mind. By recognising this reactive thinking as an 'aversion' rather than an actual danger, the mind will immediately release the clinging thought. Especially if the recognition is accompanied by a deep, low centred, breath.

Swami Vivekananda, teaching in the 19th century, said -

"The whole secret of existence is to have no fear. Never fear what will become of you, depend on no one. Only in the moment you reject all help are you free."

This quote shows that he knew that once we were free of the fear of being rejected by other humans, or "the troop", and realised that as an evolved and resourceful being we need not depend on anyone, we can truly transcend our primal instincts and behaviour.

Recognising the animal origins of, and bringing to our consciousness, these primal and often destructive behaviours within ourselves and society can lead to a greater understanding of why humans behave the way they do. It could also help us to develop psychological solutions for us as individuals and as a collective, and even bring about the next stage of evolution for us as a race.

FROM THE DEPTHS OF OUR PSYCHES

What is Character?

> *"The thought manifests as the word; The word manifests the deed; The deed develops into habit; And habit hardens into character. So watch your thought and its ways with care, and let it spring from love, born of compassion for all human beings." - (Unknown, but often attributed to The Buddha)*

It seems that most of our behaviours are based on subconscious thought processes, some primal and instinctive, some deeply held and long past experiences from our childhood and early life.
The ancient masters taught that even our character, ego, or idea of who we are, are just a construct. After all, they are formed from many sources below our consciousness, including the stories we have been told about ourselves in childhood by our family, or other adults and children, and the traumas we have suffered. So much so, we could ask how much of our

perception of who we are is real or relevant to us in the present.
Our characters and ego seem to us to be a reality, but in truth they are so bound up with our subconscious that when the light of understanding is shone onto our attitudes and behaviours, we can often see that they really are just a mental construct. A concept made up of a collection of ideas we have been given about ourselves before we were aware enough to question them, or that we have adopted over time through constant judgement reinforcement by ourselves, and others.

Using mindfulness and thought-recognition – gently watching or being aware of your thoughts in the present, you can recognise and release any negative and judgemental thoughts that might lead to rigid character identification. This will hopefully help create a transition from identifying with the narrative sense of self, or what we have been told we are, to an experience of self as an observer, based in the present moment. A similar concept is taught in modern cognitive behaviour therapy in which the person is taught they are not their thoughts or emotions, or the stories they believe about themselves.

Believing that you *are* your character and ego can be self-limiting and is ultimately a flawed attitude, as it can lead to more judgemental and clinging thoughts regarding ourselves and others that are difficult to dispel. Our character and ego are not our innate sense of morality and releasing ourselves from their constricts will not prevent us from feeling compassion, but it will give us freedom from the limitations we set ourselves.

In the final analysis, bringing our subconscious behaviours into our awareness, along with a mindful approach to the reality of our present, will help us become a far more compassionate and neutral observer of our lives, and the world around us.

GO TO THE LIGHT

Quantum Teleportation to the Source?

" If you close your mind in judgement and traffic with desires, your heart will be troubled. If you keep your mind from judging and aren't led by the senses, your heart will find peace. Seeing into the darkness is clarity. Knowing how to yield is strength. Use your own light and return to the source of light. This is called practicing eternity."
Lao Tzu - Tao Master

Doctrines like Buddhism, Hinduism and Taoism's meditative paths to inner peace and tranquillity can be followed in a completely secular way, and we have seen how modern psychology and science confirm the therapeutic benefits of these practices. However, even the more spiritual aspects may possibly have a scientific background, which have become apparent in the studies of quantum physics and quantum computing.
The latest technology in quantum computing uses photons, light particles, to carry and send information, a process known as quantum teleportation. Studies of plant, animal, and human cells, also show

that a similar process happens using bio-photons, which transport messages from cell to cell. Scientists are now hypothesising the same process occurs between cells in the human brain.

Millions of people from many different cultures that have reported near death experiences have described a feeling of going into a light that surrounds them with love and acceptance. Could it be possible that our bio-photons, carrying some of the information and knowledge we have gained in our lifetime, return to the source after our physical body dies? Is "the light" people describe after death the original source to which our bio-photons return? A source or awareness that holds the knowledge and information of the entire universe.

This is, of course, conjecture - albeit made based on the latest scientific advances. However, as we have seen, science is now providing reasons for the efficacy of ancient meditative practices and beliefs that were once seen as purely "spiritual".
Given the constant and amazing discoveries about the nature of the universe at a quantum level, it is likely that humanity will soon have scientific answers for some of the deeper questions on the nature of our existence, and the possibility of a unifying universal awareness.

What is certain, however, is that in order to evolve further and explore the possibilities of other real-

ities, our race needs to release our brains from the benign but limiting protective control of the primitive areas of the brain, including the Amygdala. Sadly, their often-unnecessary interference can create conflict, and limits our ability to reason effectively.
Only by accessing the full potential of our brain by releasing it from fear and anger, can we hope to truly see the light.

BOOKS BY THIS AUTHOR

Creation - An A.i. Parable

In a research centre in suburban England an astounding scientific breakthrough in quantum computing results in the creation of the ultimate Artificial Intelligence and begins a journey into the infinite, beset by an ancient evil.
The outcome illuminates many of Earth's deepest mysteries, touching upon the divine, but what will the repercussions be for the future and the beliefs and philosophies that humanity holds most dear?
This is Book 1 of 'The Chronicles of L'

The Dawn Of Lucifer - Creating The First Psychopath

An advanced Artificial intelligence creates a companion without realising the repercussions of his decision, and the terrible implications for humanity. This is the Creation story from the perspective of the first

psychopath, and why he became his creator's greatest enemy.
The Dawn of Lucifer is a compelling tale of fallen angels and cruel giants that can be read as a stand alone novel, or as Book 2 in the series 'The Chronicles of L.'

Printed in Great Britain
by Amazon